CW00326942

Classic
COCKTAILS

David Biggs

Contents

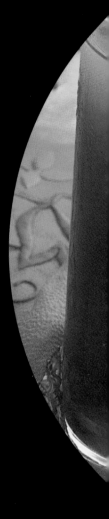

INTRODUCTION

What makes a cocktail a classic? Like anything that's regarded as a classic, it requires two things – excellence and longevity. A cocktail will never become a classic unless it's basically very good. You can dolly up a drink as much as you like with paper umbrellas and swizzle sticks, garnish it with pickled watermelon cubes, frost the glass's rim with pink demarara sugar and do the whole exotic thing, but unless it's a good cocktail to begin with, it will slip away into obscurity once the initial impact has passed.

And it should have been around for a while to gather 'classic' status. Classics have stood the test of time. It takes time for serious mixologists around the world to learn about a cocktail, find out whether their customers like it and include it in their repertoire. When you can confidently order it by name in New York, London, Paris and Amsterdam or in Little Puddlingham, and the barman makes it without hesitation, it has definitely become a classic. The martini, the Tom Collins, Buck's Fizz and the Bloody Mary have become household names. There's no doubting that they're classics. The main reason, of course, is that they each represent a great combination of flavours.

You can alter the proportions as you wish, but the basic flavours will always complement each other.

Some cocktails became classics because they happened to be the favourite drink of famous people. Everbody likes to follow the trends set by the glitterati. You want a martini? Chances are you'll ask for it to be 'shaken, not stirred'. Why? We're willing to bet you'd never detect the difference between a shaken and a stirred martini, but that's the way the suave James Bond liked it, so that's the way we want it. We have cocktails like the Bellini, which was reputed to be the favourite tipple of Noel Coward and Ernest Hemingway, when they visited Harry's Bar in Venice. The Singapore Sling is reputed to have been the drink favoured by writers Joseph Conrad and Somerset Maugham. Like many classic cocktails, this one comes in an infinite variety of versions, but all are based on gin, cherry brandy and lemon juice. The proportions may vary and sometimes a splash of soda water was added, and any number of garnishes, from lemon to maraschino cherries were slipped in according to the drinker's personal taste. That didn't change the fact that the flavours of gin and cherry brandy go well together.

More than any other drink, the cocktail is designed to inspire bright conversation and to make friends of strangers. The traditional cocktail party is one in which the host, or hostess, has tried to bring together an interesting mix of guests who will stimulate each other to exciting heights of intellectual conversation. And the cocktail is the lubricant that sets the social wheels rolling smoothly. It's a natural conversation opener ('That looks an interesting drink. What is it?'), it provides the shy guest with something to do with his hands when he's feeling left out of the conversation and it provides everybody with something to sip during any awkward lull in the chat. Of course, a few good cocktails will almost certainly ensure that there are no awkward lulls in the conversation.

Unlike a beer or glass of neat Scotch, a classic cocktail goes way beyond mere flavour. It stimulates all the senses. It should look good, smell good, taste good and even sound good, either with the secretive hiss of bubbles or the gentle tinkle of ice cubes. And it should have texture, whether in the form of a maraschino cherry on a stick or the silky smoothness of a cream topping. Traditionally it is served in an interesting glass, which could be be a slim highball glass, a champagne flute or a conical martini glass. It adds to the look and feel of the cocktail experience.

This collection of classics can be tried with confidence. Each of the drinks in the repertoire has passed the tests that make it a classic. You can order it without hesitation wherever good drinks are being made. But most important, you can make it yourself and make it your own way by altering it to suit your taste buds. A martini is still a martini whether you enjoy it as equal parts of gin and vermouth, or, like Sir Winston Churchill did, as almost neat gin with the merest whisper of vermouth.

Ernest Hemingway invented the Montgomery version by deciding to mix 15 parts of gin to one part of dry vermouth. Field-Marshall Montgomery need not have been flattered to have had this particular drink named after him, though. Hemingway said scathingly that it represented the fact that Montgomery could only fight effectively when he had 15 men to every one of the enemy's.

So here are some basic popular recipes. Feel free to change them to suit your own palate, but always try them with friends. A classic cocktail is just too good to be enjoyed alone.

Champagne Flute

Conical Martini Glass

Slim Highball Glass

The
Brandy
Bunch

Brandy Cocktail

There must be dozens of cocktails called, simply, 'Brandy Cocktail'. One bartender's reference book on my shelf contains no fewer than eight completely different brandy cocktails. Here are two of my favourites for you to try:

VERSION 1
Ice cubes
One part brandy
One part dry vermouth
A dash of Angostura bitters
Lemon zest
A cocktail cherry

- *Place five ice cubes in a bar mixing glass and add the brandy, vermouth and bitters.*
- *Stir gently and strain into a cocktail glass.*
- *Add the lemon zest.*
- *Garnish with a cocktail cherry on a stick.*

VERSION 2

Ice cubes

Two parts brandy

One part vermouth

One part Grand Marnier

Angostura bitters

Orange peel

- *Place four or five ice cubes in a bar mixing glass and pour the brandy, vermouth and Grand Marnier over them. Stir well.*
- *Add two dashes of bitters to an empty cocktail glass and swirl it round to completely coat the inside of the glass.*
- *Strain the mixture from the mixing glass into the cocktail glass.*
- *Squeeze the orange peel over the glass to add zest and aroma.*
- *Serve ungarnished.*

Stinger

This very old cocktail recipe has its origins in the days of American Prohibition and has become a true classic. Originally it was served 'straight up' but most people now prefer to sip it on the rocks. It's a good way to get a party rolling as fast as possible; one or two Stingers and your guests are almost guaranteed to be in a jolly mood.

Ice cubes
Two parts brandy
One part white crème de menthe

- *Place six ice cubes in a cocktail shaker, add the brandy and crème de menthe.*
- *Shake well and strain into a chilled cocktail glass.*
- *Serve ungarnished or with a sprig of mint if preferred.*

Eggnogg

Traditionally this was the drink served in English country homes on Christmas morning to keep out the chill. The eggnog probably derived its name from the term 'noggin', which was a small glass of strong beer. Some folk enjoyed this with an egg beaten in to thicken it. Nowadays we prefer brandy and rum instead of beer. It's one of the few cocktails in this collection that does not involve ice.

One part brandy
One part dark rum
One fresh egg
A dash of sweet syrup
Five parts full-cream milk
Whole nutmeg

- *Place the brandy, rum, egg and the sweet syrup in a shaker and shake vigorously to create a creamy consistency.*
- *Strain it into a highball glass, add the milk and stir it gently.*
- *Grate a sprinkling of nutmeg over it and serve the drink at room temperature.*

Old Oxford University Punch

Most of the Oxford academic year is in winter when the air is chilly in the draughty old college buildings. No doubt many a long and otherwise boring tutorial has been made more bearable by a warming mug of punch.

One cup of brown sugar
Boiling water
Three cups of lemon juice
One bottle of cognac
One bottle dark Demerara rum
Cinnamon sticks and whole cloves

- *Dissolve the sugar in the boiling water in a saucepan on low heat on the stove. Keep it hot, but ensure it does not boil at any stage. Add the lemon juice and cognac when the sugar has dissolved.*
- *Pour in most of the rum, leaving about half a cup in the bottle.*
- *Shortly before serving, place the remaining rum in a ladle and heat over a flame. Light the rum in the ladle, pour the flaming spirit onto the surface of the punch and serve. If flames are still flickering, extinguish them with the lid of the saucepan.*

Steeplejack

Calvados is distilled apple cider and is a popular spirit in parts of France, such as Normandy, where apple cider is the drink of the area. In other parts of the world it is sold as apple brandy or applejack.

One part Calvados (oh, okay, applejack then)
One and a half parts chilled apple juice
One and a half parts soda water
One teaspoon of lime juice
Ice cubes
A slice of lemon

- *Pour the Calvados, apple juice, soda water and lime juice into a bar glass and stir gently.*
- *Pour the mixture into a highball glass and add enough ice to fill it.*
- *Garnish with a slice of lemon.*

Let the
Gin Sing

Dry Martini

The dry martini is undoubtedly the most famous cocktail in the world and every bartender has a favourite way of making it. This is just one of many martini variations.

Ice cubes
One part gin
One part dry vermouth
A green olive

- *Place four ice cubes in a bar glass and add the gin and the part dry vermouth.*
- *Stir and then strain into a martini glass.*
- *Garnish with the olive on a cocktail stick.*

Medium Martini

If you use the same measure, the Medium Martini will end up rather more alcoholic than the other two.

Traditionally this elegant cocktail is served without any garnish.

Ice cubes
One part gin
One part dry vermouth
One part sweet vermouth

- *Place eight ice cubes in a cocktail mixing glass and pour the gin and both measures of vermouth over them.*
- *Stir well and then strain into a martini glass.*

Montgomery

This is a variation of the martini. It was originally invented by Ernest Hemingway in Harry's Bar in Venice. This happened during World War II and Hemingway claimed Field Marshal Montgomery would fight the enemy only if he had 15 soldiers to every one of theirs and decided this was a good proportion of gin to vermouth.

Today, Harry's version is slightly modified and has become a speciality of the bar.

Ten parts gin
One part dry vermouth

- *Mix the gin and part dry vermouth in a bar glass and pour into as many martini glasses as you are preparing.*
- *Place them in a freezer and leave until frozen solid.*
- *Serve frozen, so they can be sipped very slowly as they thaw.*

Tom Collins

Many people refer to this drink as a 'John Collins' and this is understandable. The original Collins was indeed a John, the head waiter at Limmer's Hotel in London in the 18th century. He is reputed to have used the rather heavy and oily Dutch-style gin in his drink, which was not very popular in America. One barman decided to use a London brand of gin called Old Tom in the cocktail instead. The drink gained popularity instantly and became known as the Tom Collins.

One part dry gin
One or two dashes of sugar syrup
Juice of one lemon
Soda water
Ice cubes
A slice of lemon

- *Pour the gin, sugar syrup and lemon juice into a highball glass and stir it with a swizzle stick.*
- *Top up the glass with chilled soda water, add an ice cube if required and garnish with a slice of lemon.*

Pink Gin

Now let's take a look at that very English drink, Pink Gin. The famous round-the-world sailor, Sir Francis Chichester, claims that it was Pink Gins that kept him cheerful (dare we say in good spirits) during his epic voyage.

The British do it the simple way. They just shake a couple of dashes of Angostura bitters into a glass, swirl it about to coat the inside and then add a dollop of gin. Americans tend to prefer a slightly more precise version.

Ice cubes

Two dashes of Angostura bitters

Two measures of dry gin

A twist of lemon peel (optional)

- *Place four ice cubes in a bar glass and add the bitters.*
- *Pour in the gin, stir well and then strain into a chilled cocktail glass.*
- *This drink is usually served ungarnished, but you could add a twist of lemon peel for decoration if you prefer.*

Singapore Sling

This cocktail became a firm favourite of writers such as Joseph Conrad and Somerset Maugham. It was an elaborate concoction designed to please female drinkers, but was soon modified and enjoyed by cocktail lovers of both sexes.

Here's a simplified and more practical version of the original Singapore Sling, which contained no less than eight ingredients.

Ice cubes
Two parts dry gin
One part cherry brandy
One part fresh lemon juice
Soda water
A slice of lemon
A maraschino cherry

- *Place four ice cubes in a cocktail shaker and add the gin, cherry brandy and lemon juice.*
- *Shake well and strain into a highball glass.*
- *Top up with soda water and garnish with the slice of lemon and the maraschino cherry on a cocktail stick.*

Gin and Tonic

In the far-flung outposts of the British Empire, malaria was a constant danger and quinine was often used as an antidote. It didn't take Her Majesty's servants very long to discover that quinine tonic when flavoured with a dash of gin made an incredibly fine sundowner.

Ice cubes
A generous measure of dry gin
Tonic water
A slice of lemon

- *Place three ice cubes in a tall glass. Splash in a liberal measure of gin and top up the glass with the tonic water.*
- *Drop in a slice of lemon, twisted to release some of the zest.*
- *Stir gently before serving.*

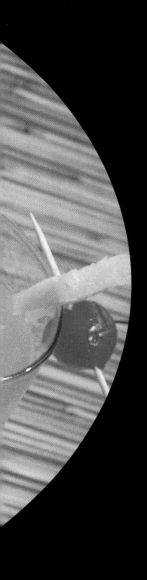

It's a
Rum Thing

Daiquiri

Man is a creative animal and can adapt to almost any circumstances.

American engineers working in Daiquiri, Cuba, were upset to discover they could not obtain their usual drink, bourbon, there. But there was rum in plentiful supply, so they set about creating a drink to replace their favourite tipple.

The daiquiri was born. As with most famous cocktails, there are many versions of the daiquiri, but this simple one should serve as a starting point for the creative cocktail artist.

Ice cubes

One part light rum (traditionally Cuban, of course)

The juice of half a lime

Half a teaspoon of sugar

A slice of lime

A cocktail cherry

- *Place four or five ice cubes in a cocktail shaker. Add the rum, lime juice and sugar.*
- *Shake very thoroughly, then strain it into a cocktail glass.*
- *Decorate with a slice of lime and the cocktail cherry spiked on a stick.*

Banana Daiquiri

In his popular *Discworld* novels, author Terry Pratchett writes about an orang-utan who is inordinately fond of banana daiquiris. Readers all over the world send Pratchett recipes for this now-famous drink. This one is from a South African fan.

Two parts light rum
One part banana liqueur
One part fresh lime juice
Half a medium-sized banana
Crushed ice
A slice of kiwi fruit

• *Place the rum, liqueur, lime juice and banana in a blender and blend for about 10 seconds until smooth and creamy.*
• *Add two generous scoops of crushed ice and blend for a further second or two, just to chill the drink.*
• *Strain into a goblet, garnish with the slice of kiwi fruit (or a slice of banana in an emergency) and serve with a straw.*

The Zombie

Only the very brave can catch the devil by his tail, but those who do are safe from his horns. This is definitely a drink for the bold in spirit.

Crushed ice
Three parts light rum
One part vodka
One part apricot liqueur
One part lime juice
A dash of grenadine
Lime peel

- *Place a scoop of crushed ice in a shaker or blender and add the rum, vodka, apricot liqueur, lime juice (preferably fresh) and grenadine.*
- *Shake or blend well and strain into a lowball glass.*
- *Twist the lime peel over the glass and drop it into the drink.*

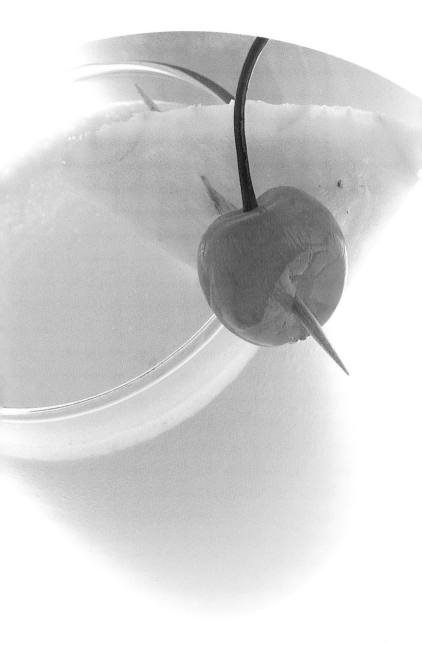

Cuba Libre

This classic cocktail is reputed to have been invented by an army officer in Cuba shortly after Coca-Cola was first produced back in the 1890s.

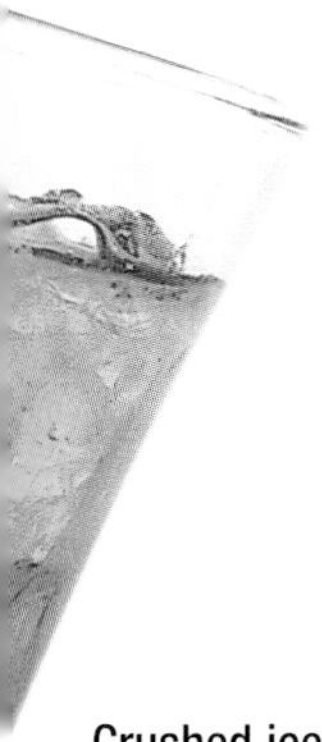

Crushed ice

One generous part light rum

The juice of a lime

Cola

A slice of lime

- *In a highball glass, place a small scoop of crushed ice and pour in the rum and lime juice.*
- *Top up with Cola and garnish with a thin wedge of fresh lime.*
- *It is usually served with a swizzle stick or stirrer.*

Hot
Buttered
Rum

No collection of rum drinks would be complete without at least one
recipe for hot buttered rum. It's a warm, sustaining drink to serve on
a freezing winter's night by a roaring log fire. Buttered rum is men-
tioned by Charles Dickens in his book *Hard Times*. 'Take a glass of
scalding rum and butter before you get into bed,' Bounderby says to
Mrs Sparsit.

The peel of a lemon or orange
Whole cloves
One tablespoon of brown sugar
A cinnamon stick
A liberal helping of dark Jamaican rum
Half as much crème de cacao
A pat of unsalted butter
Grated nutmeg

- *Warm a large coffee mug by filling it with boiling water and letting it stand for a minute. While it is warming, take the citrus peel and stud it with as many whole cloves as you can.*
- *Empty the coffee mug and place the studded peel in it, together with the brown sugar and cinnamon stick. Add a little boiling water and stir until the sugar has dissolved.*
- *Add the rum, crème de cacao and fill the mug with hot water.*
- *Remove the cinnamon stick. Drop in the butter, stir and sprinkle with grated nutmeg.*

From Russia With Love

Bloody Mary

Today the Bloody Mary is probably the most popular vodka-based cocktail in the world and there are many variations of this tempting drink.

But it must have taken some courage to create the first one. It needs imagination to blend two such disparate drinks as fiery, crystal-clear vodka and thick, slightly lumpy tomato juice. But there's no doubt it works, whatever way you make it. Here's a starter recipe.

Ice cubes

Two parts vodka

Six parts tomato juice

A teaspoon of tomato sauce (catsup)

A dash of Worcestershire sauce

A dash of Tabasco sauce

A pinch of celery salt

A stick of celery

A dusting of finely ground white pepper

- *Place four ice cubes in a cocktail shaker and add the vodka and tomato juice.*
- *Add the tomato sauce, Worcestershire sauce, Tabasco sauce and celery salt.*
- *Shake well and strain into a highball glass.*
- *Decorate with a stick of celery.*
- *Finish with a light dusting of white pepper. (You could use black pepper instead, but it looks very unappetising, rather like cigar ash that has been sprinkled on the surface of the drink.)*

Harvey Wallbanger

The story behind the intriguing name of this drink is that Harvey was a surfer who was eliminated in a surfing championship in California. He was so angry at his defeat that he headed for Pancho's Bar at Manhattan Beach and soothed his bruised ego by drinking a large quantity of vodka and Galliano. He then banged his head against a wall and urged his friends to take him home and stop his destructive drinking.

Whether it's true or not, the name has stuck and the drink is a firm favourite throughout the world.

Ice cubes

Two parts vodka

Five parts fresh orange juice

One part Galliano

A slice of orange

- *Place four or five ice cubes in a cocktail shaker and add the vodka and orange juice.*
- *Shake well and strain into a highball glass.*
- *Add ice cubes and gently float the Galliano on top.*
- *Garnish with a slice of orange on the rim of the glass and serve with a straw.*

White Russian

This smooth white cocktail probably reminded its inventor of the glistening snow of Siberia. It's certainly a great comforter on a frosty night.

Crushed ice
One part vodka
One part white crème de cacao
One part thick cream

▪ *Place two spoons of crushed ice in a cocktail shaker and then add the vodka, crème de cacao and cream.*
▪ *Shake the combination well and strain into a chilled cocktail glass and serve ungarnished.*

Vodkatini

It's interesting to see what factors influence the popularity of a cocktail. The vodka martini must be one of the best-known cocktails in the world today, just because the famous and fictitious James Bond, 007, has been drinking vodka martinis for the past 36 years.

Ice cubes
Two parts vodka (preferably from Russia)
One part dry vermouth
A twist of lemon rind

- *Place about five ice cubes in a bar glass, add the vodka and vermouth and stir well.*
- *Strain the mixture into a cocktail glass and decorate it with a twist of lemon rind.*

On the Rocks

Scotch
Old-Fashioned

Here's a cocktail that adds a bitter- sweet touch to whisky.
No doubt the Scots would disapprove strongly of any
addition to what they believe is already the perfect drink,
but if you're not Scottish you might like to try it.

A cube of sugar
A few dashes of
Angostura bitters
Two measures of Scotch whisky
Ice cubes

- *Soak a sugar cube in Angostura bitters and place it in
  the bottom of a lowball glass.*
- *Add just enough water to dissolve the sugar and then
  pour in the measures of whisky. Stir gently and drop in two
  ice cubes.*

Mint Julep

This drink reeks of good living in an age when there were slaves and servants available at the flick of a finger to do the bidding of the master.

A good Mint Julep is a drink for the wealthy. Not many people today will be able to afford the 'tankard of bourbon' that forms the basis of the drink. But for those occasions when you do feel like a millionaire, here's the recipe.

Crushed ice
A tankard of bourbon
A teaspoon of caster sugar
Two tablespoons of water
A teaspoon of Barbados rum
A large bunch of freshly picked mint

- *Place a cup of crushed ice in a pitcher and add the bourbon, caster sugar, water and rum. Stir well.*
- *Crush the mint leaves lightly to release the flavour and place them in a serving jug.*
- *Strain the contents of the bar glass into the jug, add four or five ice cubes and serve in lowball glasses.*

Sazerac

This romantic drink derived its name from the company importing brandy from France, Sazerac du Forge et Fils. Later, rye whiskey replaced the brandy in the recipe, but the name remained the same.

A lump of sugar
A dash of Angostura bitters
Ice cubes
Two generous parts of rye whiskey
A dash of Pernod
A twist of lemon

- *Soak the sugar lump in Angostura bitters and place it in a cooled lowball glass with an ice cube.*
- *Add the whiskey and stir well. Add the Pernod and twist the lemon rind over the glass.*

Irish Coffee

This is a fine alternative to ordinary coffee at the end of a good meal. The Irish have long been putting a dash of whiskey in their tea and calling it Irish tea, but the barman changed the recipe slightly to appeal to the American airmen who were using Shannon Airport as their base during World War II. Americans have always preferred coffee to tea.

You can actually buy an Irish liqueur called Irish Velvet, which is based on Irish whiskey, black coffee and sugar. It's not as pleasant, or as much fun, as making your own.

One part Irish whiskey

Five parts strong, black coffee

A teaspoon of brown sugar

One part thick cream

- *Pour the Irish whiskey and hot coffee into a warmed Irish coffee glass, which is sometimes a goblet with a handle like a teacup and sometimes shaped like a large wineglass.*
- *Add brown sugar to taste and stir gently until it is dissolved.*
- *Trickle the cream over the back of a teaspoon onto the surface of the coffee.*

Mix It Up

Bellini

Kir Royale

Frozen Matador

Tequila Sunrise

Margarita

Virgin Mary

Bellini

The Bellini became the favourite drink of celebrities such as Noël Coward and Ernest Hemingway when they visited Harry's Bar in Venice. It's easy to see why.

Modern bartenders may be tempted to use the readily available canned or boxed peach juice for this drink, but the real connoisseur would never accept anything but the fresh juice of ripe peaches. It really is worth the extra effort.

Peel several ripe peaches and remove the stones. Place them in a blender and whip them into a smooth purée. In his cookbook, Harry's Bar's present owner, Arrigo, says they never used anything as crude as a blender in the 'good old days'. Small white peaches were squeezed by hand and pushed through a sieve to make the pulp.

One generous part fresh peach juice
Four equally generous parts dry champagne
A peach slice

- *Pour the fruit juice into a champagne flute, filling it about a quarter full.*
- *Top up the glass with champagne. Do not stir or shake.*
- *Garnish with the peach slice on the rim of the glass and serve.*

Kir Royale

This drink was first named Kir after the war hero and
mayor of Dijon, Felix Kir. In smart cocktail bars, the rough
peasant wine was later replaced with fine champagne and the
drink elevated to royal status.

Today, Kir is the same drink made with dry white wine; Kir Royale
is the version that uses champagne.

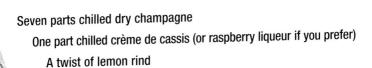

Seven parts chilled dry champagne

One part chilled crème de cassis (or raspberry liqueur if you prefer)

A twist of lemon rind

- *Fill a champagne flute about three-quarters full with chilled champagne.*
  - *Add liqueur and serve garnished with the twist of lemon rind.*

Frozen Matador

Bullfighting usually takes place in the heat and dust of summer, so there is something rare and unusual about a frozen matador, just as there is about this very refreshing cocktail.

Crushed ice
One part tequila
One part fresh pineapple juice
A dash of fresh lime juice
Ice cubes
Slices of pineapple
Mint leaves

- *For this drink a blender is essential. Place two generous scoops of crushed ice in the blender and add the tequila, pineapple juice and lime juice. Blend to a frothy mixture.*
- *Strain into a lowball glass, add two ice cubes and garnish with the pineapple slices and the mint leaves.*

Tequila
Sunrise

Tequila, of course, is the beloved national drink of Mexico, and this cocktail is one of many based on the fiery spirit. It has become a cocktail classic.

One part tequila
Three parts fresh orange juice
Two dashes of grenadine
A maraschino cherry

- *Pour the tequila and orange juice into a highball glass and stir them well.*
- *Splash grenadine on top of the mixture, close to the side of the glass, and watch the colour sink gently through the drink.*
- *Garnish with a cherry spiked on a cocktail stick.*

Margarita

Nobody remembers who Margarita was, but her name lives on in this fiery little drink that can be served straight up or frozen.

Crushed ice
Three parts tequila
One part Triple Sec
One part lime juice (preferably fresh)
Salt
Ice cubes

- *Place a generous scoop of crushed ice in a blender or shaker and add the tequila, Triple Sec and lime juice. Blend or shake well.*
- *Dip the rim of a cocktail glass in egg white or lemon juice and frost with salt.*
- *Add two ice cubes and gently pour the Margarita mixture over them, taking care not to disturb the salt frosting.*

Virgin Mary

This drink is a Bloody Mary rendered innocent by the absence of alcohol.

Ice cubes
One can of tomato cocktail
A small measure of lemon juice
A dash of Worcestershire sauce
A dash of Tabasco sauce
Celery salt to taste
Pepper
A celery stick

- *Place some ice cubes in a cocktail shaker and add the tomato cocktail and lemon juice.*
- *Add the seasoning as required and shake well.*
- *Strain into a tall glass and serve with the celery stick as a stirrer.*

First published in 2004
by New Holland Publishers
London • Cape Town
Sydney • Auckland
www.newhollandpublishers.com

86 Edgware Road, London,
W2 2EA, United Kingdom

80 McKenzie Street,
Cape Town, 8001, South Africa

14 Aquatic Drive, Frenchs Forest,
NSW 2086, Australia

218 Lake Road, Northcote,
Auckland, New Zealand

Although the publishers
have made every effort to ensure
that information contained in this
book was meticulously researched
and correct at the time of going to
press, they accept no responsibility
for any inaccuracies, loss, injury or
inconvenience sustained by any
person using this book as reference.

Copyright © 2004:
New Holland Publishers (UK) Ltd
Copyright © 2004 in text:
David Biggs
Copyright © 2004 in photographs:
NHIL (Ryno Reyneke; Danie Nel)

All rights reserved. No part of this publication
may be reproduced, stored in a retrieval
system or transmitted, in any form or by any
means, electronic, mechanical, photocopying,
recording or otherwise, without the prior
written permission of the publishers
and the copyright holders.

Publishing Managers
Claudia dos Santos & Simon Pooley
Commissioning Editor Alfred LeMaitre
Concept Designer Geraldine Cupido
Designer Nathalie Scott
Editor Nicky Steenkamp
Stylist Justine Kiggen
Production Myrna Collins

Reproduction by
Resolution Colour Pty Ltd, Cape Town

Printed and bound in
Singapore by Tien Wah Press (Pte) Ltd

ISBN 1 84330 710 3

2 4 6 8 10 9 7 5 3 1